ULSTER

AN ILLUSTRATED YEARBOOK
1993

ULSTER

AN ILLUSTRATED YEARBOOK
1993

Illustrations

Terry Aston · Leo Duff · David Evans
James MacIntyre · Joanna Martin
Colin Maxwell · Marcus Patton

Text · Marcus Patton

Appletree Press

First published by The Appletree Press Ltd, 19-21 Alfred Street, Belfast BT2 8DL. Illustrations © Terry Aston, Leo Duff, David Evans, James MacIntyre, Joanna Martin, Colin Maxwell, Marcus Patton, 1992. Text © Marcus Patton, 1992. Printed in the EC. All rights reserved. No part of this publication may be reproduced or transmitted in any form or by any means, electronic or mechanical, photocopying, recording or in any information or retrieval system, without prior permission in writing from the publishers.

Front cover: Royal Avenue, Belfast (Terry Aston)
Back cover: Parish Church, Ballintoy,
   Co. Antrim (Leo Duff)

Endpapers (front): Schoolhouse and Barbican,
      Glenarm, Co. Antrim (Colin Maxwell)
   (back): Ross's, May Street, Belfast
      (Terry Aston)

ISBN 0 86281 347 6

List of Illustrations

Meter House, Ormeau Road, Belfast *week*	1
Ocean Buildings, Donegall Square, Belfast	2
Public Library, Armagh	3
Bridewell, Magherafelt, Co. Londonderry	4
Gospel Hall, The Mall West, Armagh	5
La Belle Epoque, Great Victoria Street, Belfast	6
Model Newsagent, Bessbrook, Co. Armagh	7
Gresham Arcade, North Street, Belfast	8
General View, Londonderry	9
Cottage near Bellarena, Co. Londonderry	10
General View, Armagh	11
Houston's Mill, Broughshane, Co. Antrim	12
Scrabo Tower, Co. Down	13
Hilltown, Co. Down	14
Walker Seeds, Newtownards, Co. Down	15
St Patrick's Cathedral (RC), Armagh	16
Stormont, Belfast	17
Quaker Meeting House, Grange, Co. Tyrone	18
Monea Castle, Co. Fermanagh	19
The Brass Rail Bar, Buncrana, Co. Donegal	20
Former Market House, Draperstown, Co. Londonderry	21
King's Hall, Belfast	22
McAuley's Hotel, Carnlough, Co. Antrim	23
Royal Avenue, Belfast	24
Gate Lodge, Sion Mills, Co. Tyrone	25
Clachan at Fair Head, Co. Antrim	26
Ulster Folk and Transport Museum, Cultra, Co. Down	27
Parish Church, Ballintoy, Co. Antrim	28
Culraney, Co. Antrim	29

	week
Ardress House near Loughgall, Co. Armagh	30
Holy Trinity Church, Ballycastle, Co. Antrim	31
Ice Cream Shop, Warrenpoint, Co. Down	32
Spur Royal, Augher, Co. Tyrone	33
Cottage near Carndonagh, Co. Donegal	34
Scally's Drapery Shop, Ballycastle, Co. Antrim	35
Former Police Station, Dungannon, Co. Tyrone	36
Cottages in Silent Valley, Co. Down	37
House in Strangford, Co. Down	38
Bandstand, Forthill Park, Enniskillen, Co. Fermanagh	39
Strandtown Primary School, Belfast	40
Bangor Abbey, Bangor, Co. Down	41
The Hermitage, Tolleymore, Co. Down	42
Eel Fishery, Toomebridge, Co. Antrim	43
Bushmills, Co. Antrim	44
The Diamond, Londonderry	45
Carrickfergus Castle, Co. Antrim	46
Former Restaurant, Castle Place, Belfast	47
Jordan's Castle, Ardglass, Co. Down	48
Red Bay Castle, Co. Antrim	49
The Guildhall, Londonderry	50
Nendrum, Mahee Island, Co. Down	51
Castle Coole, Enniskillen, Co. Fermanagh	52
Church of the Sacred Heart, Omagh, Co. Tyrone	53

Contributors

Terry Aston

Terry Aston was born near Manchester and studied at Manchester and Leicester Colleges of Art. He taught at Sunderland Polytechnic before coming to Belfast in 1969. At present he teaches drawing and illustration in the Faculty of Art and Design at the University of Ulster. He also works on commissioned drawing and illustration, and has exhibited in the USA as well as in several Belfast galleries.

Leo Duff

Leo Duff was born in Belfast, educated at Victoria College and subsequently studied at Brighton College of Art and the Royal College of Art Illustration School. She has exhibited widely with one-man shows in Belfast, Dublin and London, and group exhibitions in Britain, Ireland and the USA. Her work appears in many public collections, including the Victoria and Albert Museum, as well as the private collections of, among others, Mary Robinson and Sir Terence Conran.

David Evans

Born and educated in Belfast, David Evans is a lecturer in architecture at Queen's University. As a water-colourist he concentrates on landscape and architectural subjects. He has exhibited at the Bell, Gordon and Octagon galleries and is currently President of the Royal Ulster Academy of Arts. Other interests include architectural conservation, and he is co-author, with Marcus Patton, of *The Diamond as Big as a Square* (1981).

James MacIntyre

Born in Coleraine, James MacIntyre lived and worked in London for many years before returning to settle in Co. Antrim. He held his first one-man exhibition in Belfast in 1945 and since then has exhibited widely and regularly. His work also appears in many public collections, among them the Ulster Museum, Queen's University, Belfast, the Arts Council of Northern Ireland and the BBC.

Joanna Martin

Joanna Martin was brought up in Holywood, Co. Down and studied book illustration and graphic design at Edinburgh College of Art. She has worked full time in graphic design from 1984-1991, six years of which were in London. In 1991 she set up her own business in Newtownards under the title The Attic Studio and since then has been involved in a wide range of projects related to illustration and graphics. Other examples of her work can be seen in *Irish Blessings,* published by Appletree Press in 1992.

Colin Maxwell

Colin Maxwell was born and educated in Belfast. An architect, he works in private practice in the city. He exhibits in local galleries and has held one-man exhibitions at the Octagon Gallery and at the Royal Society of Ulster Architects.

Marcus Patton

Marcus Patton was born in Enniskillen and studied architecture at Queen's University, Belfast. He works for Hearth, a housing association specialising in the restoration of historic buildings, and is also a prolific illustrator of architectural and musical subjects. He is a Fellow of the Society of Architectural Illustrators and an Associate of the Royal Ulster Academy.

Introduction

Every schoolboy knows that a historical document is a musty piece of vellum stored under humidity-controlled conditions in a record office, and occasionally brought out under heavy security for a blockbuster exhibition at a museum. Of course, there are many different types of historical documents, ranging from wills to acts of parliament, and from letters to the proverbial laundry lists, but not all records exist on paper, and many of the most vivid are actual artefacts that have come down to us from earlier times. The range of these is enormous, from furniture and clothes to tools and utensils. But perhaps the most accessible of all to the student of local history are the buildings of our ancestors. They aren't locked away in museums or private collections, but line the streets we walk along every day.

Although the history told by buildings is easy to see, it is by no means a complete record. If the old buildings of Ulster had been bound up into a history-book, there would be a surprising richness of information in some pages, but, frustratingly, many other pages would have been torn out, while others would have been obliterated or even, rather mysteriously, rewritten.

The architectural history-book of Ulster begins well, with a rich heritage of pre-Christian raths and standing stones. Many of the early Christian sites have also come down to us, albeit remains like Nendrum (*see week 51*) are little more than foundations, and the great monastery at Bangor (*see week 41*), "the head of so many monasteries, a place truly sanctified, and so fruitful in saints" as St Bernard wrote, had been reduced by 1610 to "vast walls of white stone", all but a fragment of which has now gone. Nevertheless, it takes only a little imagination to picture what Nendrum at least must have been like, since its setting surrounded by the waters of Strangford Lough has changed remarkably little. The old walls were not swallowed up by the earth, of course — the handsomely faced and carved stones were no doubt "salvaged" by local farmers and recycled in their own houses.

The next few pages of our architectural book seem to consist of partially erased chapter headings, with very little text: we have inherited a considerable number of plantation tower-houses or castles, built by the English and Scottish settlers at the beginning of the seventeenth century, but practically none of the ordinary houses that must have existed at the same time. The reason for this is simply that the castles were built of stone and designed to withstand the onslaughts of their enemies, whereas many of the houses were built with timber frames, like the half-timbered houses that can still be seen in the south of England. These succumbed to the attacks of the native Irish, notably during the 1641 uprising, and perhaps also to the much damper climate of Ireland, which is so conducive to timber rot. As for the cottages of the native Irish themselves, many of these were built of mud with thatched roofs, and once they were vacated and the thatch had collapsed, the mud walls were washed away within a generation. In some areas, rough fieldstone was used for the walls, and such ruins do survive when they have not been cleared to make way for replacement dwellings. Even the castles, which probably originally had thatched roofs, are now mostly roofless and in ruins, but Monea (*see week 19*) and Jordan's Castle (*see week 48*) provide impressive evidence of the determination and courage of those early settlers.

There are some beautiful illustrations in the chapters dealing with the eighteenth century, the Georgian era. Many of them are of properties now belonging to the National Trust, like Castle Coole (*see week 52*) and Ardress (*see week 30*). These tend again to be the residences of the gentry, who could afford to use the best materials and highest standards of craftsmanship, and whose ancestors continued to care for their buildings. By this time, however, Ulster was a reasonably civilised place, with linen merchants developing early industry and building comfortable houses, perhaps similar to the Lismacloskey thatched house in the Folk Museum (*see week 27*). The evidence of ordinary houses, however, is again rather patchy, this time because the Victorians didn't like the look of Georgian houses much and tended to alter or demolish them during the following century. As a result, many pages of elegant or simply picturesque buildings have been torn out of our book.

The plot thickens in the Victorian era, which seems to consist of endless flashbacks like an arty film. There are memories of the baronial castles — is the Dungannon Police Station (*see week 36*) not a recollection of that earlier character at Monea? — puzzling references to English or even French Gothic churches from the Middle Ages, as at Omagh (*see week 53*), while office blocks like the Ocean Buildings (*see week 2*) confusingly appear disguised as Perpendicular cathedrals. You have to have your wits about you in this chapter, which is a bit like reading *War and Peace*, there are so many different characters and events to keep track of.

There are some pages here that have been rubbed out and rewritten, often using rather flowery prose. The Victorians took a keen interest in antiquities, but thought they could improve on them by restoring them as they might have been if the original builders had known as much as they did. This well-intentioned but often misguided approach was a bit like rewriting Bach for the electric guitar and throwing in a few additional variations. It was criticised at the time by William Morris and his associates as being destructive of all the ancient character of old buildings, but led to the drastic alteration of many fine buildings here as well as in England. The vigorous crudity of earlier work was regularly cut out and replaced by often excellent craftsmanship that was, however, much more mechanical in its approach.

Towards the end of the book it seems as if a child has scribbled over a lot of the pages, and again a lot have been torn out. The twentieth century has seen an attempt to build a new architecture without reference to the past, and it has resulted in some pretty crude buildings, much as a child would produce with building blocks and no training in the different ways buildings can be put together. What is worse, it has been necessary to pull down so many fine buildings of earlier eras to make way for them. Furthermore, the imposition of a road system to suit the private car and the heavy lorry, and the demand for faster and cheaper ways of building have caused immense destruction.

Although this general line of development can be traced in most areas of the province, the architectural "documents" vary in content from one part to another. The historical record of country areas is always more complete than that of urban areas, where space is at a premium and the same site may have been reused several times. Ironically, this has meant that remote tower-houses abandoned in the seventeenth century have often survived, while those that gave rise to prosperous towns, like the original Belfast Castle, were destroyed long ago. At the heart of most towns and villages there was probably originally a "clachan", or small group of cottages, but these only survive in isolated areas like Fair Head (*see week 26*). However, some towns do retain features of great antiquity, like the mediaeval road layout of Downpatrick, and the hilltop Cathedral of Armagh (*see week 11*).

As with any good read, there are some red herrings planted in the text to confuse the casual reader — the odd date-stone transplanted from one building to another of a later date, or a plaque that refers to the foundation of an institution rather than of the building. Sometimes, too, the clues can be hard to decipher, or when deciphered give rise to further questions, like clues in a treasure hunt. If you look carefully, you can often see where a building has been extended, or old windows have been blocked up. If alterations are carried out in character, they can be nearly invisible, but too often they stick out like a sore thumb.

People often boast about how old their house is — usually either ''a hundred years old'', or dating from ''about 1690''. This may mean that the structure of the walls dates from about that time, yet when you look at the house your gaze meets pebble-dashed walls, artificial slates, plastic windows with fake glazing bars, a new hardwood front door, a low modern fireplace, and all the accoutrements of the Dallas or Eldorado life. It is no more like an old house than a Chippendale chair with the legs replaced in different timber, seat reupholstered in dralon, and the back reveneered in plastic is like an antique. Such a house is no longer the historic document it may so recently have been, and it might just as well have been pulled down and replaced.

Of course, repairs are necessary, and from time to time even replacement of the elements of a building are required. In particular, if a building changes use alterations are usually required, but when they are done in a gradual and careful manner they are integrated into the building and become part of its history. Buildings cannot just be regarded as museum pieces and they cannot be preserved as meticulously. We can expect the Elgin Marbles to remain unchanged as long as the British Museum holds onto them, but when we look at an old building it is only in essence the structure that was put up one to two hundred years ago — its windows will have been repainted many times, mortar joints renewed several times, and the very stone and bricks may have decayed and acquired a new character in the process. But the process of ageing is not unattractive; buildings, like people, gain venerability and character as they get older, and the wrinkles can actually add to their richness.

This yearbook is a trawl through some of these old documents: rather a random one, since each artist has picked his or her own favourite buildings across the province, but in its small compass it does give a flavour of the tremendously varied architectural heritage of Ulster and of the activities of its inhabitants, from the early Christian monks to the Plantation settlers, from the small farmers to the wealthy businessmen of late Victorian Belfast. The story is still going on — there are some very glossy pages at the end of our little history-book, the ink hardly dry on them — and there are other pages still to be filled . . .

Marcus Patton

ULSTER

AN ILLUSTRATED YEARBOOK
1993

1992-93 DECEMBER-JANUARY

Monday • Week 1 — 28
Great day with all the family except Mark and Valerie who are in Scotland. Grandchildren performed well. Meal was good. Paula with us for first Christmas season. Gladys was also present. Sadie not so well. Powders from Eddie for her.

Tuesday — 29
Went to Martin's at Gracehill for evening with the Mucklecroft Family, Catherine, Martin R & Sadie. Lovely evening. Nice house. Played Tarot then discussed Biblical matters. Late home. Sadie feeling better. Finished powders. Sat with Philip & Paula for a while before retiring.

Wednesday — 30
Went to baby sit for Margaret. Had Grandmother to near died passing. Home and out to meeting. Study in Philemon. Fair turn out. Good pray time. Home with Sadie & Catherine. Supper & bed 12.25 AM.

Thursday — 31
Afternoon took Wed to Budget DIY. Bought society for flues. Jim Paisley & Boys called for Ashley. Went to watchnight service. Read the heart by. Bill spoke on Psalm 136. Ian & Craig testimony. Finished up Lily's work at Coleraine until Fri. Philip & Paula were at Coleraine until Fri.

Margaret's Granny died 31st Dec.

Friday / New Year's Day / Bank & public holiday — 1
Did some writing in the morning. Went with Sadie to Abbey Centre & carpet lands etc. Had tea in Skandia Howard St. Called at Paul's. Saw Margaret & children. Paul was working till Sat. Home & cup of coffee. Philip & Paula were home. Philip left Paula home in Sadie's car.

Saturday — 2
Went with Sadie to N. Ards market. Shops. Carpet.

Bands.

Sunday — 3
Service = Morn = Rev 3 Philadelphia. Even = S of S. C2. Afternoon. Lily's (sister) for supper with Lily Porter.

METER HOUSE
Ormeau Road, Belfast
(Colin Maxwell)

The Belfast gasworks, which opened in 1823, was one of the first in the United Kingdom, and it became so successful that its profits are said to have funded the building of the City Hall at the turn of the century. This little building was known as the Middle Section Meter House and was topped with an ornamental fish-scale patterned dome that has recently been taken down for restoration. Gas production stopped in 1978, and Northern Ireland is now one of the few countries in Europe without a proper piped gas supply.

1993 JANUARY

Monday • Week 2 — 4
Went with Ivan to Ballywatts fo Billy.
O.B. Meeting. Bill John Harold Sam David & Self.

Tuesday — 5
At Tillies Mothers Funeral. Then to Ballywatts fo Billy. Roy in worked at Rubs etc of Car.

Wednesday — 6
At Ballygowan Fix Flags etc.

Thursday — 7
Ivan Major for Bible Study. Commenced Killeston Job. Went to see Mrs Rankin at 24 Florida Dr. Went to photocopy at Church with Cathers.

Friday — 8
At Killeston

Saturday — 9
Steam Evening.
Went to Doulls with Beelroles. Went with Sadie to Gourdys Carpets took Ashleigh; went to ORMC Playgrounds. Went to Supervise.

Sunday — 10
Jean Chapman.
Lilys & Self fo.

OCEAN BUILDINGS
Donegall Square, Belfast
(Leo Duff)

Elderly Victorians must have wondered what their world was coming to as they watched the demolition of the old Georgian houses of Donegall Square being replaced by turretted iron-framed skyscrapers, like this one erected in 1902. Designed by Young & Mackenzie for the Ocean Accident Guarantee Corporation, this is covered with richly detailed carvings of animals cavorting in foliage, and the heads of kings and queens, along with mermaids which were the Ocean's trademark.

1993 JANUARY

Monday • Week 3 — SCAFFOLDING NOT AVAILABLE FOR KIRKISTOWN. Home for day. Call from agent to say House can be viewed in the evening (Patterson). **11**

Tuesday **12**

Wednesday **13**

Thursday **14**

Friday **15**

Saturday **16**

Sunday **17**

PUBLIC LIBRARY
Armagh
(Marcus Patton)

Having been founded in 1771, with the collection of Archbishop Robinson as its nucleus and an inscription in Greek over the entrance, this is no ordinary public library. For blockbusters there are shelves of sermons, for thrills the memoirs of Elizabethan explorers; and the busts of Robinson and the later Archbishop Beresford cast a severe eye on the proceedings. Interspersed with the books are cabinets of coins, bronze axe-heads and bones, giving the atmosphere of a slightly eccentric museum.

1993   **JANUARY**

Monday • Week 4

18

Tuesday

19

Wednesday

20

Thursday

21

Friday

22

Saturday

23

Sunday

24

**BRIDEWELL
Magherafelt,
Co. Londondery
(Colin Maxwell)**

Magherafelt was founded during the Plantation by the Salters' Company in 1609, but this bridewell, or gaol, despite a heavy iron gate in a stone archway and a stout timber door, is only a mock fortification dating from 1804. It has recently been converted into a heritage centre.

1993   **JANUARY**

Monday • Week 5   **25**

Tuesday   **26**

Wednesday   **27**

Thursday   **28**

Friday   **29**

Saturday   **30**

Sunday   **31**

**GOSPEL HALL
The Mall West, Armagh
(Terry Aston)**

This must be the most ornate gospel hall in Northern Ireland, but then it started life in 1884 as a masonic hall. Come to think of it, it must have been the most ornate masonic hall in the province: the basic hall is ornamented with a crow-step gable, a ventilator topped with a tall, thin fleche, a low round tower for the staircase, and a taller square tower. The whole is decorated in striped brickwork and commands a view of Armagh's green Mall.

1993   **FEBRUARY**

Monday • Week 6

1

Tuesday

2

Wednesday

3

Thursday

4

Friday

5

Saturday

6

Sunday

7

**LA BELLE EPOQUE
Great Victoria Street,
Belfast
(Joanna Martin)**

In the mid nineteenth century, Great Victoria Street was a fashionable road lined with dignified three-storey houses, many of which fell into disrepair because of road blight in the 1960s. This was built in 1868 as part of a block known as Prince Arthur Terrace, most of which has now been demolished. Occupied in the 1880s by a piano dealer, it was in flats by 1920, and in the 1970s was a bookshop. A few years ago it became a French restaurant, and this Muchaesque mosaic of bustled Empire ladies was affixed to it.

1993 FEBRUARY

Monday • Week 7 — **8**

Tuesday — **9**

Wednesday — **10**

Thursday — **11**

Friday — **12**

Saturday — **13**

Sunday — **14**

**MODEL NEWSAGENT
Bessbrook, Co. Armagh
(Colin Maxwell)**

John Grubb Richardson established the village of Bessbrook in 1845 to house the workers at his linen mill, and it was to inspire the more famous English model villages of Saltaire and Bournville. As a Quaker, Richardson ensured that Bessbrook had neither pubs nor pawnbrokers. The family were great innovators: in 1883 Bessbrook was running trams to Newry, only two years after the first electric tram in the world was established in the USA.

1993 FEBRUARY

Monday • Week 8 **15**

Tuesday **16**

Wednesday **17**

Thursday **18**

Friday **19**

Saturday **20**

Sunday **21**

**GRESHAM ARCADE
North Street, Belfast
(Terry Aston)**

North Street was the main commercial street of early nineteenth-century Belfast, crammed with shoemakers, tallow-chandlers, umbrella-makers, grocers, publicans and tobacco manufacturers, squeezed into the length of the street, some of them living down the twenty or so narrow entries off it. Many of the more prestigious firms moved into Royal Avenue when it was built nearby in the 1880s, opening up "development opportunities" for other businesses. Gresham Arcade, with its ornamental iron gateway, was built about 1895.

1993   **FEBRUARY**

Monday • Week 9   **22**

Tuesday   **23**

Wednesday   **24**

Thursday   **25**

Friday   **26**

Saturday   **27**

Sunday   **28**

**GENERAL VIEW
Londonderry
(David Evans)**

Although its history goes back to a monastic settlement in the sixth century, the core of Derry today is the walled city surrounding the cathedral and the formal streets laid out by the London Companies in 1614. The city walls are of earth faced with rubble stonework and are about twenty feet high and up to thirty feet wide, pierced by seven gates. By the end of the eighteenth century, the city had expanded beyond the walls, and the construction of a bridge over the Foyle permitted the development of the Waterside area during the nineteenth century.

1993   **MARCH**

Monday • Week 10   **1**

Tuesday   **2**

Wednesday   **3**

Thursday   **4**

Friday   **5**

Saturday   **6**

Sunday   **7**

**COTTAGE NEAR BELLARENA
Co. Londonderry
(Marcus Patton)**

In most parts of Ulster, thatch is held in place by wooden scallops bedded into turf, but in coastal north Derry and Donegal the exposed conditions led to the development of a different technique known as roped thatch. In this little stone cottage near Magilligan the ropes criss-cross the thatch and are fixed to projecting stones at the gable, battening the hatches down for the next Atlantic storm.

1993   **MARCH**

Monday • Week 11   **8**

Tuesday   **9**

Wednesday   **10**

Thursday   **11**

Friday   **12**

Saturday   **13**

Sunday   **14**

**GENERAL VIEW
Armagh
(David Evans)**

Armagh is the ecclesiastical capital of Ireland. The hill above the town, once a pagan fort, is now crowned by the Church of Ireland cathedral, said to have been founded by St Patrick, and the twin spires of the Catholic cathedral appear to the left. Curving round the hilltop are the fine Georgian houses of Vicar's Hill on the left, Whaley's Buildings with their tall bow windows, and an excellent recent scheme by the Housing Executive.

1993   **MARCH**

Monday • Week 12

15

Tuesday

16

Wednesday
*St Patrick's Day
Bank holiday*

17

Thursday

18

Friday

19

Saturday

20

Sunday

21

**HOUSTON'S MILL
Broughshane,
Co. Antrim
(Colin Maxwell)**

At one end of the trim little town of Broughshane one of its most interesting buildings lies empty and neglected. Unlike many mills, this one still has the water supply that once powered its machinery, a stream that bubbles down a small waterfall behind the large trees and winds past the main gable of the mill towards the town. At the turn of the century there were six mills in the area for scutching flax, beetling linen and grinding corn.

1993   **MARCH**

Monday • Week 13   **22**

Tuesday   **23**

Wednesday   **24**

Thursday   **25**

Friday   **26**

Saturday   **27**

Sunday   **28**

**SCRABO TOWER
Co. Down
(Leo Duff)**

Standing 134 feet high on its hilltop at the head of Strangford Lough, Scrabo Tower can be seen for many miles around and is one of the best-known landmarks in the province. It is a monument to the 3rd Marquis of Londonderry, a noted pistol duellist who had risen to become adjutant-general to the Duke of Wellington, and was known as the Fighting Marquis. The tower was designed by Sir Charles Lanyon and built in 1858 using basalt and local sandstone.

1993   **MARCH-APRIL**

Monday • Week 14 **29**

Tuesday **30**

Wednesday **31**

Thursday **1**

Friday **2**

Saturday **3**

Sunday **4**

**HILLTOWN
Co. Down
(David Evans)**

Appropriately named, Hilltown is situated at a crossroads in the heart of the Mourne country and enjoys spectacular views of the nearby mountains — Craigdoo, Spelga, Hen Mountain, Cock Mountain, and Eagle Mountain being the nearest. As well as its markets providing a focal point for local shepherds, Hilltown is popular with hill-walkers and anglers.

1993   **APRIL**

Monday • Week 15

5

Tuesday

6

Wednesday

7

Thursday

8

Friday
Good Friday
Bank holiday

9

Saturday

10

Sunday
Easter Day

11

**WALKER SEEDS
Newtownards,
Co. Down
(Joanna Martin)**

Until quite recently, many streets of small eighteenth- and nineteenth-century stone houses had survived intact in Newtownards, giving it a distinctively Scottish character that is fast disappearing. Although no longer domestic, this building is a remnant of the tiny single-storey houses that lined many of the old streets, often flanked by two-storey neighbours that had been "riz up" alongside. The colourful window display here includes paintpots that have strayed in from the paintshop next door.

1993   **APRIL**

Monday • Week 16   **12**
Easter Monday
Bank & public holiday

Tuesday   **13**

Wednesday   **14**

Thursday   **15**

Friday   **16**

Saturday   **17**

Sunday   **18**

ST PATRICK'S CATHEDRAL (RC)
Armagh
(Terry Aston)

Armagh's second cathedral was built in the mid nineteenth century on a hilltop with grand Italianate steps leading up to it. Started in 1840 by Thomas Duff, work was suspended during the Famine and completed in 1873 by J. J. McCarthy. Every available surface inside is decorated with mosaic, formerly culminating in intricate marble work at the altar; this was removed following recent liturgical changes and has been replaced by incongruous modern sculptures.

1993   **APRIL**

Monday • Week 17   **19**

Tuesday   **20**

Wednesday   **21**

Thursday   **22**

Friday   **23**

Saturday   **24**

Sunday   **25**

STORMONT
Belfast
(Colin Maxwell)

When the province of Northern Ireland was set up, two major public buildings were planned, both of which were designed by English architects in neo-classical style using white Portland stone: the Law Courts in Chichester Street and the Parliament buildings at Stormont, designed by Sir Arnold Thornely and opened in 1932. Stormont has a spectacularly formal straight driveway nearly a mile long that rises to the great steps of the Parliament buildings.

1993   **APRIL-MAY**

Monday • Week 18   **26**

Tuesday   **27**

Wednesday   **28**

Thursday   **29**

Friday   **30**

Saturday   **1**

Sunday   **2**

QUAKER MEETING HOUSE
Grange, Co. Tyrone
(Marcus Patton)

In keeping with their simple creeds, the Quakers built this eighteenth-century meeting house near Moy in very plain style using local red sandstone rubble. Nevertheless, it is a place of great peace, with mature beech trees sheltering the modest uniform gravestones, and only the cawing of crows in the old trees breaking the silence.

1993 MAY

**MONEA CASTLE
Co. Fermanagh
(Terry Aston)**

Most of the Plantation period tower-houses or castles built in Ulster in the early seventeenth century concentrated on strength and defensibility rather than ornament, which makes Monea Castle, built by Malcolm Hamilton about 1620, rather unusual. Its entrance is flanked by two circular towers that culminate in crow-stepped gables, and both the castle and its defensive bawn are reasonably intact today.

Monday • Week 19
Bank & public holiday — **3**

Tuesday — **4**

Wednesday — **5**

Thursday — **6**

Friday — **7**

Saturday — **8**

Sunday — **9**

1993   **MAY**

Monday • Week 20

10

Tuesday

11

Wednesday

12

Thursday

13

Friday

14

Saturday

15

Sunday

16

**THE BRASS RAIL BAR
Buncrana, Co. Donegal
(Leo Duff)**

The main street of Buncrana still has a considerable number of buildings erected during its heyday as a seaside resort, although many are now converted to amusement arcades or modernised pubs. The Brass Rail Bar, with its smooth-rendered ground floor and chrome-faced lettering, brings a taste of 1950s America to the busy street.

1993   **MAY**

Monday • Week 21

17

Tuesday

18

Wednesday

19

Thursday

20

Friday

21

Saturday

22

Sunday

23

FORMER MARKET HOUSE
Draperstown,
Co. Londonderry
(Colin Maxwell)

The merchant companies of London retained their interest in Ulster long after the Plantation, and in 1818 the Drapers' Company decided to develop the hamlet of Ballynascreen into a stylish new classical town. The central squares of Ulster villages, which are usually known as Diamonds, can take a variety of shapes, and this Market House, built in the 1830s and now converted into a library, commands a uniquely triangular square.

1993   **MAY**

Monday • Week 22

24

Tuesday

25

Wednesday

26

Thursday

27

Friday

28

Saturday

29

Sunday

30

**KING'S HALL
Belfast
(Leo Duff)**

Every year the farming community of Northern Ireland makes its pilgrimage to this modernistic reinforced concrete shed on the outskirts of Belfast to view the latest fashions in agricultural equipment and gauge the quality of beef and mutton on display. Although the Balmoral Show is the main event in the calendar of the King's Hall, this 1933 building, with its dramatic art-deco facade, is also a venue for rock concerts and trade exhibitions throughout the year.

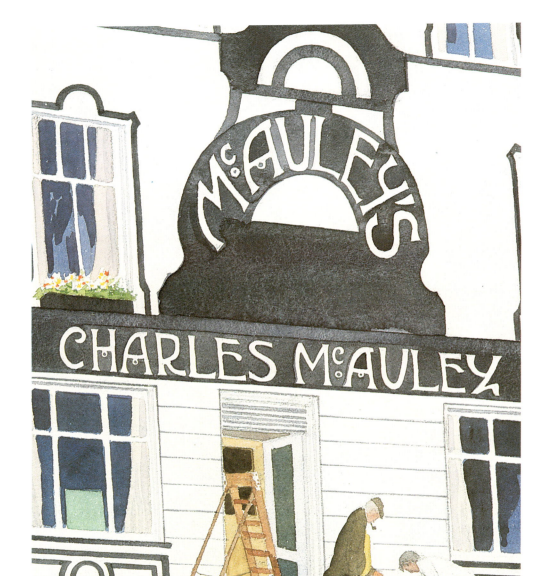

1993 **MAY-JUNE**

Monday • Week 23
Bank holiday

31

Tuesday

1

Wednesday

2

Thursday

3

Friday

4

Saturday

5

Sunday

6

**McAULEY'S HOTEL
Carnlough, Co. Antrim
(James MacIntyre)**

Although painted with a restricted palette of black and white, this splendid art-nouveau gable is one of the most spectacular hotel fronts along the Antrim coast, marrying the elegance of its flowing lettering with the brashness of its more modern seaside-resort neighbours. Inside is an unpretentious but hospitable pub.

1993   **JUNE**

Monday • Week 24   **7**

Tuesday   **8**

Wednesday   **9**

Thursday   **10**

Friday   **11**

Saturday   **12**

Sunday   **13**

ROYAL AVENUE
Belfast
(Terry Aston)

In this view the City Hall is viewed from Castle Place, with the corner of Anderson & McAuley's department store topped by its rooftop clock, the red sandstone Bank Buildings of 1900 and, caught in a shaft of sunlight, the Reform Club on the right. The Bank Buildings were built as a department store but get their name from one of the city's first banks that formerly had its premises on the site.

1993 **JUNE**

Monday • Week 25 **14**

Tuesday **15**

Wednesday **16**

Thursday **17**

Friday **18**

Saturday **19**

Sunday **20**

GATE LODGE
Sion Mills, Co. Tyrone
(Leo Duff)

Sion Mills is a mill village, laid out with long terraces of houses built for workers at the Herdman's spinning mill. However, it is the neo-Tudor Sion House and its associated gate lodge and stable building which make the village particularly remarkable. Built about 1850 by W. F. Unsworth, the architect of the first Shakespeare Memorial Theatre at Stratford-on-Avon, these give the village a unique charm, and it is sad to see them currently so neglected.

1993   **JUNE**

Monday • Week 26
21

Tuesday
22

Wednesday
23

Thursday
24

**CLACHAN AT FAIR HEAD
Co. Antrim
(James MacIntyre)**

Clachans, or isolated groups of small cottages, are now rare in the province, although formerly they were as common as villages. Sheltered below the crest of Fair Head, this cluster of half a dozen cottages, many now derelict, displays the characteristically random arrangement of such hamlets. Nearby is a remarkably well-preserved crannog, or man-made fortified island, in the Lough na Crannog.

Friday
25

Saturday
26

Sunday
27

1993 JUNE-JULY

Monday • Week 27　　**28**

Tuesday　　**29**

Wednesday　　**30**

Thursday　　**1**

Friday　　**2**

Saturday　　**3**

Sunday　　**4**

**ULSTER FOLK AND TRANSPORT MUSEUM
Cultra, Co. Down
(Marcus Patton)**

It sometimes seems as if there are more thatched cottages in the Folk Museum than are still left "in the wild"; the visitor here can see everything from this rather grand two-storey example down to a modest weaver's cottage. A reconstructed Ulster town as it might have been at the turn of the century is gradually materialising, and every year new buildings from all parts of Ulster are reconstructed here, now including a church, a printer's shop and a schoolhouse.

1993   **JULY**

Monday • Week 28   **5**

Tuesday   **6**

Wednesday   **7**

Thursday   **8**

Friday   **9**

Saturday   **10**

Sunday   **11**

PARISH CHURCH
Ballintoy, Co. Antrim
(Leo Duff)

Whether the sea behind is grey and stormy or calm and blue, the solid roughcast walls of Ballintoy's parish church stand out on the edge of its headland as a haven of calm and meditation. Simple and brightly whitewashed, with tiny windows in the spiky battered tower, and firmly rooted in its stone-walled graveyard, this looks like the ecclesiastical equivalent of the Irish thatched cottage.

1993 JULY

Monday • Week 29
Bank & public holiday
12

Tuesday
13

Wednesday
14

Thursday
15

Friday
16

Saturday
17

Sunday
18

**CULRANEY
Co. Antrim
(James MacIntyre)**

Set precariously on the steep hillside north of Cushendun is a narrow, winding road that skirts the Antrim coast, with the Mull of Kintyre seeming a very short distance away across the North Channel. Culraney is centred on a small cluster of white buildings including the church with its bell tower and the tiny village schoolhouse behind it. The school is currently threatened with closure as its roll is down to only ten pupils, but what the Culraney scholars might lose on the standard curriculum, they surely more than make up in the searingly beautiful setting of their academy.

1993   **JULY**

Monday • Week 30   **19**

Tuesday   **20**

Wednesday   **21**

Thursday   **22**

Friday   **23**

Saturday   **24**

Sunday   **25**

ARDRESS HOUSE NEAR LOUGHGALL Co. Armagh (Marcus Patton)

Once a simple manor house, Ardress was grandified by its late eighteenth-century owner, George Ensor, who extended its front elevation by adding a literal facade at each end. Despite such theatrical devices, however, Ardress is a charming house with turkeys gobbling in its farmyard, an immaculate flower garden and, like many houses in Co. Armagh, an extensive apple orchard.

1993   **JULY-AUGUST**

Monday • Week 31   **26**

Tuesday   **27**

Wednesday   **28**

Thursday   **29**

Friday   **30**

Saturday   **31**

Sunday   **1**

**HOLY TRINITY CHURCH
Ballycastle, Co. Antrim
(Joanna Martin)**

The parish church of Ballycastle was built in 1756 in a rather naive classical style, with the Venetian window and doorcase not quite in scale with the heavy tower. On the side of the tower is a sundial for use on cloudless days, and on the front is a large clockface for use the rest of the year. The generally simple interior of the church is set off by a pretty Victorian decorated pipe organ.

1993   **AUGUST**

**ICE CREAM SHOP
Warrenpoint, Co. Down
(Marcus Patton)**

In the eighteenth century, Italian families brought fine plasterwork to Irish houses; in the nineteenth century, Italians fleeing the wars of independence against France and Austria again settled in Ireland, many working as musicians or establishing cafés that made ice cream. The Magliocci family founded this business in 1910, and their house and shop on the large square at Warrenpoint, with its intricate pale-blue bargeboard and the hand-painted lettering for "Ices" is in the very best tradition of seaside resorts.

Monday • Week 32   **2**

Tuesday   **3**

Wednesday   **4**

Thursday   **5**

Friday   **6**

Saturday   **7**

Sunday   **8**

1993　　　　　AUGUST

Monday • Week 33　　　**9**

Tuesday　　　**10**

Wednesday　　　**11**

Thursday　　　**12**

Friday　　　**13**

Saturday　　　**14**

Sunday　　　**15**

**SPUR ROYAL
Augher, Co. Tyrone
(David Evans)**

Although situated on the edge of Augher town, the castle looks over a very private and tranquil lake. The original castle, known as "Spur Royal", was built by Sir Thomas Ridgeway in the early seventeenth century to an unusual star-shaped plan. It fell into ruin, but was restored and extended in the early nineteenth century with a new Gothic mansion house topped by castellations and corner turrets.

1993 **AUGUST**

Monday • Week 34

16

Tuesday

17

Wednesday

18

Thursday

19

Friday

20

Saturday

21

Sunday

22

COTTAGE NEAR CARNDONAGH
Co. Donegal
(James MacIntyre)

One of the charms of traditional cottages is the way the outbuildings and "lean-tos" group around the house, sometimes at an odd angle dictated by cramped field boundaries or the contours of the ground. Too often, even on the Inishowen peninsula, modern bungalows with their shallow roofs and large plain windows are replacing the subtleties of the old cottages.

1993 AUGUST

Monday • Week 35

23

Tuesday

24

Wednesday

25

Thursday

26

Friday

27

Saturday

28

Sunday

29

SCALLY'S DRAPERY SHOP
Ballycastle, Co. Antrim
(Terry Aston)

Ballycastle is probably most widely known for the Auld Lammas Fair which takes place each year at the end of August, but if you actually want to see its shops it is best to visit the town during the rest of the year. Scally's drapery shop, one of many attractive traditional shopfronts in the village, is set in a Georgian house that straddles the steep hill of Castle Street with one leg longer than the other.

1993   **AUGUST-SEPTEMBER**

Monday • Week 36
Bank holiday

30

Tuesday

31

Wednesday

1

Thursday

2

Friday

3

Saturday

4

Sunday

5

FORMER POLICE STATION
Dungannon, Co. Tyrone
(Marcus Patton)

The market square at the centre of Dungannon is set on the slope of a steep hill that was the castle of the O'Neills for nearly 400 years. In 1871 this tall stone fortress was erected there — due to the error of a clerk in Dublin, so the story goes, who sent plans for the Dungannon police station to the Khyber Pass and Indian plans to Co. Tyrone. It's a good story, but the crow-stepped design is really thoroughgoing Scottish baronial, with the addition of steel-doored gunloops commanding each corner, no doubt to repel Fenians rather than Hindoos.

1993   **SEPTEMBER**

Monday • Week 37   **6**

Tuesday   **7**

Wednesday   **8**

Thursday   **9**

Friday   **10**

Saturday   **11**

Sunday   **12**

COTTAGES IN SILENT VALLEY
Co. Down
(James MacIntyre)

This small cottage and its cluster of whitewashed outbuildings are set on the lower slopes of the Mourne Mountains near the Silent Valley, snuggling closely into the hillside and sheltered by a few trees. All around are the local drystone walls built of rounded granite boulders that look like stacks of giant potatoes.

1993   **SEPTEMBER**

Monday • Week 38   **13**

Tuesday   **14**

Wednesday   **15**

Thursday   **16**

Friday   **17**

Saturday   **18**

Sunday   **19**

HOUSE IN STRANGFORD
Co. Down
(Colin Maxwell)

This house is at the western end of the village of Strangford, which wraps itself in steep tiers around its small bay at the entrance of Strangford Lough. Nearby is a house decorated with scallop shells and coloured glass. With the ferry constantly plying between it and Portaferry on the other side of the Strangford narrows, and yachts and other craft moored offshore or coming in to the stone piers, the village has the constant activity of a small harbour, but without any feeling of commercialisation.

1993   **SEPTEMBER**

Monday • Week 39

20

Tuesday

21

Wednesday

22

Thursday

23

Friday

24

Saturday

25

Sunday

26

BANDSTAND, FORTHILL PARK
Enniskillen,
Co. Fermanagh
(Marcus Patton)

The visitor to Enniskillen sees from a distance the steep mound of Forthill Park and a tall column peeping over its trees, on which stands the statue of General Sir Galbraith Lowry Cole, second son of the 1st Earl of Enniskillen. It is possible to climb to the top for a spectacular view. In front of the monument is an ornamental octagonal bandstand, erected as a memorial to Thomas Plunkett, a late nineteenth-century town commissioner.

1993   SEPTEMBER-OCTOBER

Monday • Week 40	**27**
Tuesday	**28**
Wednesday	**29**
Thursday	**30**
Friday	**1**
Saturday	**2**
Sunday	**3**

**STRANDTOWN PRIMARY SCHOOL
Belfast
(Colin Maxwell)**

Modern architecture was slow to come to the province, and most new buildings of the 1930s were in the neo-Georgian style, often using rustic brick and small-paned windows. The twenty-six new schools built by the Belfast Education Board between the wars under the direction of the architect R. S. Wilshere, such as Strandtown School completed in 1930, although determined to bring sunshine, ventilation and cheerfulness into the classroom in the best modern manner, are in many ways unashamedly classical.

1993 OCTOBER

Monday • Week 41 — **4**

Tuesday — **5**

Wednesday — **6**

Thursday — **7**

Friday — **8**

Saturday — **9**

Sunday — **10**

**BANGOR ABBEY
Bangor, Co. Down
(Terry Aston)**

This church marks the location of one of the most important early Christian settlements in the British Isles, from whence during the Dark Ages Irish monks travelled all over the known world. The monastery founded by St Comgall in 558 and rebuilt by St Malachy had fallen into ruin by 1367, and a new church built at that time was burnt in 1572, after the Dissolution of the Monasteries. The present building incorporates the tower of the fifteenth-century church, but was otherwise rebuilt in the early nineteenth century.

1993 OCTOBER

Monday • Week 42

11

Tuesday

12

Wednesday

13

Thursday

14

Friday

15

Saturday

16

Sunday

17

**THE HERMITAGE
Tolleymore, Co. Down
(Marcus Patton)**

Tolleymore Forest Park extends over some 1,200 acres centred on the valley of the Shimna River. In the eighteenth century the grounds were ornamented with fanciful gateways and eccentric bridges by Lord Limerick and his son Lord Clanbrassil. This extraordinary hermitage, which looks at first sight little more than a pile of stones perched over a deep pool, was built in the 1770s, complete with Gothic openings and a stone bench. Any hermit taking up residence today would still find the place as damp and picturesque as he could wish.

1993   **OCTOBER**

Monday • Week 43

18

Tuesday

19

Wednesday

20

Thursday

21

Friday

22

Saturday

23

Sunday

24

**EEL FISHERY
Toomebridge,
Co. Antrim
(Colin Maxwell)**

Izaak Walton considered that eels were probably bred "either of dew, or out of the corruption of the earth". The truth is just as strange: eels breed near the Sargasso Sea, and the tiny elvers swim back across the ocean, arriving in their millions at the mouth of the Bann and other estuaries. These swim to freshwater lakes to mature before returning to the breeding grounds where they die. Many, however, are caught in this elaborate permanent fishing net at the northern end of Lough Neagh.

1993   **OCTOBER**

Monday • Week 44   **25**

Tuesday   **26**

Wednesday   **27**

Thursday   **28**

Friday   **29**

Saturday   **30**

Sunday   **31**

BUSHMILLS
Co. Antrim
(James MacIntyre)

Bushmills, which has recently been declared a conservation area, is celebrated for the whiskey distillery that was first licensed to make whiskey in 1608, but the River Bush also powered mills for making paper, flour and spades, and it retains many attractive and well-to-do houses from the eighteenth and nineteenth centuries. Here the classical doorcase and spear-headed railings contrast with the rustic whitewashed wall on the other side of the road.

1993 NOVEMBER

Monday • Week 45 **1**

Tuesday **2**

Wednesday **3**

Thursday **4**

Friday **5**

Saturday **6**

Sunday **7**

**THE DIAMOND
Londonderry
(Terry Aston)**

The Diamond is a square at the centre of the walled city of Derry, dominated by the tall Edwardian department store of Austin's, with its large plate glass windows supported by highly ornamented columns and topped by a fishscale copper dome. In the centre stands the First World War Memorial built in 1927, with vigorous sculptures of a soldier on one side, and on the other a bare-footed seaman of "HMS *Derry*", apparently brought onto deck in an emergency and struggling to get his sea-jacket on.

1993   **NOVEMBER**

Monday • Week 46   **8**

Tuesday   **9**

Wednesday   **10**

Thursday   **11**

Friday   **12**

Saturday   **13**

Sunday   **14**

CARRICKFERGUS CASTLE
Co. Antrim
(David Evans)

Just over 800 years ago John de Courcy started building the castle at Carrickfergus, and it was continuously garrisoned until 1928. It last saw military action when 800 French troops under Thurot attacked it in 1760. The defendants used the buttons off their tunics when they ran out of other ammunition, and when they eventually capitulated the French allowed them to march out retaining their swords and colours. However, the invaders had lost too much time and retreated to sea, where their ships were later taken or sunk off the Isle of Man.

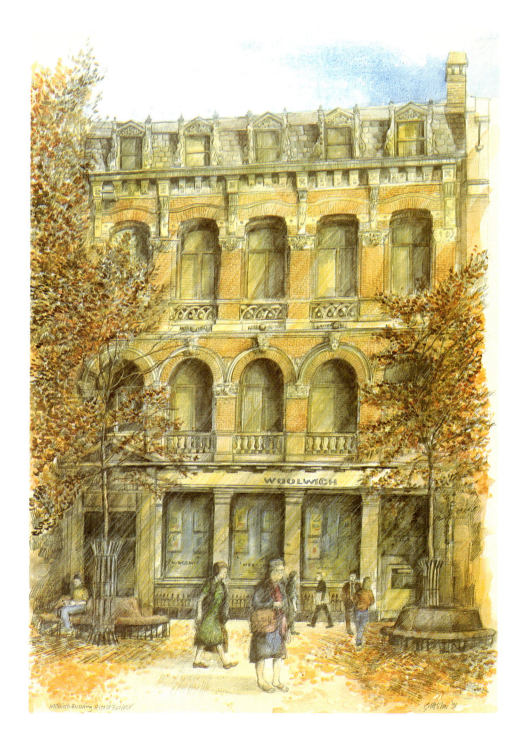

1993   **NOVEMBER**

Monday • Week 47   **15**

Tuesday   **16**

Wednesday   **17**

Thursday   **18**

Friday   **19**

Saturday   **20**

Sunday   **21**

**FORMER RESTAURANT
Castle Place, Belfast
(Terry Aston)**

One of the more eccentric architects of Victorian Belfast was William Hastings, who designed a number of highly ornate buildings in the city, including this restaurant erected in 1866. The fairly simple basic structure here is overlaid with writhing carvings of plants, that would not be out of place on a much later building, and culminate in the mansard roof with its quirky dormer windows. The ground floor is a later addition.

1993 NOVEMBER

Monday • Week 48 **22**

Tuesday **23**

Wednesday **24**

Thursday **25**

**JORDAN'S CASTLE
Ardglass, Co. Down
(David Evans)**

For a small town, Ardglass is extremely well-off for fortifications, having no less than seven castles within its boundaries. To be sure, some are fairly small structures, two are nineteenth-century follies and one is now a golf club, but it's still a tally few towns can compete with. Jordan's Castle is probably the best preserved castle and dates back to the fifteenth century, when Simon Jordan was besieged here for three years by the Earl of Tyrone's forces. Today the four-storey tower is in state care.

Friday **26**

Saturday **27**

Sunday **28**

1993 NOVEMBER-DECEMBER

Monday • Week 49

29

Tuesday

30

Wednesday

1

Thursday

2

Friday

3

Saturday

4

Sunday

5

**RED BAY CASTLE
Co. Antrim
(Leo Duff)**

Just along the coast from Waterfoot, the Antrim Coast Road winds round a headland, passing under a tall arch of red conglomerate as it does so, and on the crown of the hill above squats the ruin of a sixteenth-century castle built by the Macdonnells. It was burnt by Shane O'Neill in 1565, was rebuilt and used till about 1640, and has since weathered down like a melting candle to become almost part of the rock itself.

1993   **DECEMBER**

Monday • Week 50 — **6**

Tuesday — **7**

Wednesday — **8**

Thursday — **9**

Friday — **10**

Saturday — **11**

Sunday — **12**

THE GUILDHALL
Londonderry
(Terry Aston)

Situated on the quayside just outside the city walls is the Gothic sandstone Guildhall. Burnt out in 1908, it was rebuilt to a more elaborate style by 1912; it was again burnt in 1972 but has since been restored. The elaborate great hall inside is widely used for festivals and even for plays.

1993   **DECEMBER**

Monday • Week 51

13

Tuesday

14

Wednesday

15

Thursday

16

NENDRUM
Mahee Island, Co. Down
(Marcus Patton)

Although it consists of little more than ruins and the stump of a round tower, Nendrum is the most complete surviving early monastic settlement in Northern Ireland, and a visit to this gentle, hilly peninsula in the maze of small islands that make up the western side of Strangford Lough gives a vivid impression of what life for the early monks must have been like. They lived in beehive huts, the circular foundations of which can be seen here, and three stone walls protected the church, while a round tower would have given advance warning of Viking raids.

Friday

17

Saturday

18

Sunday

19

1993   **DECEMBER**

Monday • Week 52

20

Tuesday

21

Wednesday

22

Thursday

23

**CASTLE COOLE
Enniskillen,
Co. Fermanagh
(Leo Duff)**

Friday
Christmas Eve

24

Generally regarded as one of the finest classical mansions in Ireland, Castle Coole on the outskirts of Enniskillen was built for the 1st Earl of Belmore in the 1790s to designs by James Wyatt. It was constructed of pristine Portland stone that was brought across from England by sea and canal at great expense, but its chaste neo-classical style, with unblinking windows in plain surrounds, makes it seem severe rather than lavish.

Saturday
Christmas Day

25

Sunday
Boxing Day

26

1993-94 DECEMBER-JANUARY

Monday • Week 53
Bank & public holiday
27

Tuesday
Bank & public holiday
28

Wednesday
29

Thursday
30

Friday
31

Saturday
New Year's Day
1

Sunday
2

CHURCH OF THE SACRED HEART
Omagh, Co. Tyrone
(Terry Aston)

Omagh started life with a monastery and a fort, as befits its hilltop location. Today the centre of the town is dominated by the classical Courthouse, which faces down the main street, and William Hague's extraordinary Church of the Sacred Heart, whose two lop-sided towers can be seen from all over the town. Inside, the church has a long nave with a hammerbeam roof springing from corbels carved as heads of saints.

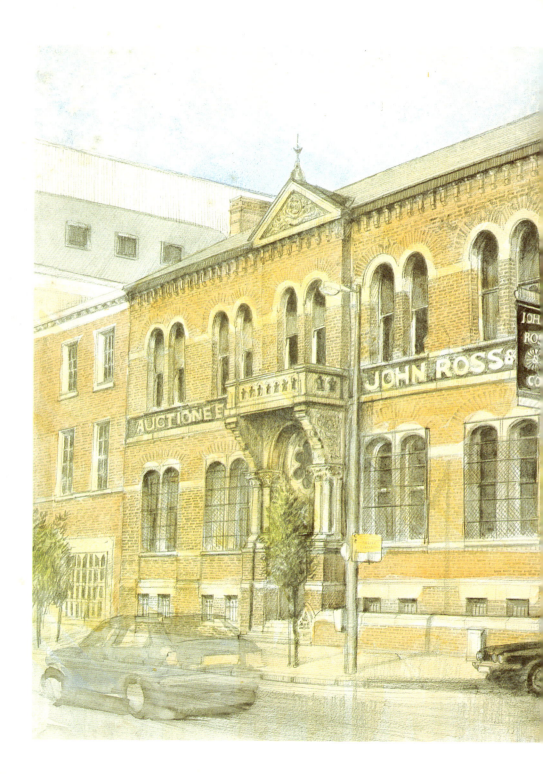